RAILWAYS AROUND BEDFORDSHIRE

John Jackson

AMBERLEY

First published 2023

Amberley Publishing
The Hill, Stroud
Gloucestershire, GL5 4EP

www.amberley-books.com

ISBN 978 1 3981 0896 7 (print)
ISBN 978 1 3981 0897 4 (ebook)

British Library Cataloguing in Publication Data.
A catalogue record for this book is available from
the British Library.

Origination by Amberley Publishing.
Printed in the UK.

Contents

Introduction

The county of Bedfordshire witnesses thousands of motorists passing through it every day, with both the M1 and A1 running broadly north to south through the county. The same applies to rail travellers. Most long-distance passengers realise that both the Midland Main Line and the East Coast Main Line pass through the county. Less well known, the West Coast Main Line also has a short stretch of railway track within the county's boundaries in the Leighton Buzzard area.

These three major rail arteries serve ten passenger stations that survive within the county. In addition, a branch line linking Bedford to Bletchley, within the Milton Keynes urban area, has also survived into the twenty-first century. Known as the Marston Vale line, the branch line serves a further eight Bedfordshire communities. This brings today's total number of passenger stations in Bedfordshire to eighteen.

Of course, like any other county, Bedfordshire suffered from line and station closures in the last century, primarily as a consequence of the infamous Beeching Report published in the 1960s. A total of twenty-five stations within the county were closed, ranging from wayside halts on the county's main arteries to more substantial line closures. Towns such as Dunstable, with a population today of around 35,000 people, were deprived of any rail service whatsoever.

Other line casualties included the branch westwards through Turvey towards Northampton, and the line south-eastwards through Shefford and Henlow towards Hitchin. Back in the nineteenth century, this latter route was the railway's means of reaching London from Leicester through an interchange at Hitchin, until construction of today's route from Bedford through Luton.

In this publication, however, we concentrate on the railways that have survived. Around 700,000 people currently live in the county, with half of these within the two major towns. These are Luton, with around 250,000 residents and Bedford, the county town, with approximately 100,000. For the last decade or so, Bedford has also been my home.

With both of these towns being within easy commute of London, it is the service to the capital that forms the backbone of Midland Main Line stopping services in the county. The line from London St Pancras was electrified as far north as Bedford in the 1980s. Since then, electrification has progressed northwards through Wellingborough and Kettering and on to Corby.

As well as Luton and Bedford, the county has intermediate stations on this route at Flitwick, Harlington and Leagrave. It also has a station to the south of Luton, called Luton Airport Parkway, opened in 1999 and serving the airport itself, around a mile away. London Luton Airport station is around 30 miles from central London, a similar distance to that of Gatwick Airport to the south.

At the same time as the electrification to the north of Bedford, the reinstatement of previously removed tracks has resulted in a four-track railway throughout from Kettering to London. This has led to more flexibility in scheduling for both passenger and freight services. Slower moving freight services can now move in both directions without both using a single 'slow line' for bi-directional purposes or impeding the movement of their faster passenger counterparts.

Beyond Kettering, the Midland Main Line offers passengers regular services to Leicester, Derby, Nottingham and Sheffield. At the time of writing, these services remain diesel-hauled throughout, with a decision on further electrification to the north still very much in the balance.

To the south of the county, the reopening of London's Snow Hill tunnels has enabled through running of passenger services between Bedford and Luton to Gatwick Airport and Brighton. To accommodate these services the low-level platforms at St Pancras International were opened in 2007, replacing King's Cross Thameslink on the nearby Pentonville Road.

A similar cross-London service now links the three Bedfordshire stations on the East Coast Main Line, at Sandy, Biggleswade and Arlesey, with these same platforms at St Pancras International, as part of a regular through service between Peterborough, the city of London and Horsham, in West Sussex.

By contrast, the West Coast Main Line (WCML) has seen electric power through the county since the 1960s, with four tracks throughout between London Euston and the junction at Hanslope, to the south of Northampton. The WCML skirts the western boundary of the county of Bedfordshire around Leighton Buzzard. The station here serves the town together with nearby Linslade and is around 40 miles from London's Euston terminus. It is served by regular passenger services between the capital and Milton Keynes Central, Northampton and onwards to Birmingham.

Until closure under the Beeching Act in 1965, Leighton Buzzard was also a junction station for services to Dunstable and beyond, towards Luton. The track between Leighton Buzzard and Dunstable was removed, although the section between Dunstable and the Midland Main Line saw freight traffic until the early 1990s. Some of this trackbed is now in use as part of the Luton and Dunstable busway. The town is also home to a narrow gauge railway that runs for approximately 3 miles, operating from a station at Page's Park to the south of the town.

As already mentioned, these three main lines through Bedfordshire enjoy varying levels of freight traffic, most of which passes on longer-distance workings. A variety of examples of these are demonstrated in the chapters that follow.

Three local freight destinations are worthy of mention. Freight facilities on the Midland Main Line continue to be provided at both Elstow, just to the south of Bedford, and at Luton, where two unloading locations remain in use. In addition, on the East Coast Main Line, Plasmor are a longstanding customer of the railways, using the former goods yard at Biggleswade station for delivery of their concrete-based products.

The final passenger line within the county is the branch linking Bedford to Bletchley, to the south of Milton Keynes. This service, formerly part of the so-called Varsity line linking Oxford and Cambridge, escaped closure under the Beeching Act. The ongoing threat of closure remained, however, and on 1 January 1968 much of the route closed, leaving only the localised Bedford to Bletchley section open for passenger traffic.

Since then, a section to the west between Oxford and Bicester has reopened with a fully reinstated rail link, under the East West Rail branding, remaining on the horizon to again link the two university cities of Oxford and Cambridge. Plans are in their infancy and, in this publication, I make no attempt to pre-empt what may or may not happen. Suffice to say, the Marston Vale chapter in this publication focuses on the local service that is on offer today. Regrettably, the line is the subject of regular rail replacement bus service substitutions, with a variety of reasons for such being offered.

As a regular user of this convenient link line, I can say it is particularly disappointing to witness the experiences of customers frustrated by the lack of continuity or reliability of a passenger train service. Nevertheless, we feature the local branch trains in recent years, together with some of the non-passenger workings using this connection between Midland Main Line and West Coast.

Our journey round the county commences in the east with the East Coast Main Line and continues broadly from east to west, concluding with the county's short stretch of West Coast Main Line.

As always, I hope that you enjoy browsing through the pages that follow as much as I have enjoyed compiling them.

Bedfordshire Passenger Railway Map

This map shows today's passenger railways that run through the county of Bedfordshire. As can be seen, the East Coast Main Line, Midland Main Line and West Coast Main Line all pass through the county. The Marston Vale branch, running broadly north-east to south-west, links Bedford to Bletchley with a number of stations continuing to serve rural, scattered communities along the route. The passenger stations that remain open within the county are highlighted in green.

East Coast Main Line

Three passenger stations remain open on the Bedfordshire stretch of the ECML, with the most northerly of these being at Sandy. The town's station lies approximately 44 miles from the London terminus of the ECML at King's Cross, opened as part of the Great Northern Railway in 1850. This photo shows the station buildings and entrance today.

These station buildings are on the far left of this scene at Sandy station in 2018. The view, looking north towards Peterborough, shows the two-platform station on a four-track railway, with each platform now extended to take a twelve-coach train.

3 miles to the south lies the town of Biggleswade. Its station was also opened in 1850, when the line was double-track. It was rebuilt at the turn of the twentieth century to enable a four-track railway to be constructed, together with its current two island platform configuration. This is the view looking south towards London in September 2020.

To the south of Biggleswade station, the remaining sidings are used by the Plasmor Brick Company. This is the scene in September 2020, with a rake of their wagons having been unloaded and awaiting movement later that afternoon.

The third Bedfordshire ECML station is at Arlesey, a further 4 miles to the south of Biggleswade. The original station for the town was closed to passengers in 1959 and the buildings subsequently demolished. The station was reopened in 1988 at the time when stopping services on the line were operated by Network South East. This is the new two-platform station in November 2017, looking north towards Peterborough.

On the southern fringes of Arlesey is the site of the former station of Three Counties. The station, closed in 1959, was so called because of the nearby Three Counties Asylum. The latter was a joint venture between Bedfordshire, Huntingdonshire and Hertfordshire, hence its Three Counties name. Little trace of the demolished station exists, as evidenced in this scene from November 2020. The asylum was also known as Fairfield Hospital.

The county's other closed station on the ECML was at Tempsford, to the north of Sandy. The level crossing remains in use here, although it was earmarked for replacement by an alternative vehicle access bridge several years ago. This view looking south from here shows the former cattle pen and goods shed. The station itself opened in 1863 and was closed in 1956.

The East West Rail Consortium seeks to reinstate the Varsity line between Oxford and Cambridge, originally closed in 1968. The Central Section of this project involves crossing the ECML, probably to the north of Tempsford, and onwards to Cambourne and Cambridge via a completely new route. One of the best surviving stations on the former route is at Potton, 3 miles to the east of Sandy. The platforms and buildings, seen here in April 2021, remain mainly intact and are now in private ownership.

The ECML has seen a number of different passenger operators since the national rail privatisation in the mid-1990s, particularly on its longer-distance InterCity services. Space precludes giving a full historic account of these operators for the last thirty years. A cross-section of passenger services follows in the next few pages. On 3 September 2013, East Coast-liveried 91121 heads through Biggleswade on a northbound service.

The Class 91 electric locomotives had entered service between 1988 and 1991 with thirty-one locos working services between London Kings Cross and Yorkshire, Newcastle and Edinburgh. On 8 May 2016, 91117 passes Tempsford crossing, unusually at the London end of this southbound service. By this time, services were being operated by Virgin Trains East Coast.

On 8 September 2020, 91124 is seen passing the site of Three Counties station on a northbound express. These services had changed operators again by this date, having been placed in the hands of Department for Transport in 2018, operating services under the London North Eastern Railway (LNER) branding.

Later the same day, sister loco, 91114, is seen approaching Holme Green crossing, south of Biggleswade. The use of Class 91 loco-hauled services is being phased out as their Azuma replacements enter service.

The Class 91 locos operate with a Driving Vehicle Trailer (DVT) at the opposite end of the train. The formation is usually formed with the DVT at the London end of the service, with the Class 91 at the north, or country, end of the train. This means that all southbound services are usually powered by the Class 91 propelling from the rear. This is the case on 13 July 2020 with DVT numbered 82211 leading this London Kings Cross service through Tempsford.

In order to provide cover for their own Class 91 locos, East Coast operators have frequently hired in Class 90 electric locomotives from DB Cargo. On 5 September 2018, for example, 90036 is seen passing Tempsford on a LNER service from London Kings Cross to Newark North Gate.

The high-speed train (HST) was first introduced on East Coast Main Line services in May 1978. These Class 43 locos and coaching stock were to notch up over forty years' service before being replaced by the next generation of units, the Azumas. On 19 November 2017, 43319 leads 43316 through Arlesey on a London Kings Cross to Edinburgh service.

Heading in the opposite direction through Tempsford on 4 August 2018 is 43274. These diesel units operate as far north as Aberdeen and Inverness. This power car was, however, named *Spirit of Sunderland* in December 2015, recognising the first anniversary of direct services from that city to the capital.

The East Coast fleet of HST sets was often supplemented by sets hired in from the then Midland Main Line operator, East Midlands Trains. On 25 September 2017, power car 43061 leads 43076 on a southbound working to Kings Cross.

Competitive services on the East Coast Main Line include workings from London to both Bradford and Sunderland operated by Grand Central. Until the end of 2017 the company had a small fleet of these much-loved HSTs on its books. On 19 November 2017, their power car, 43467, leads a Kings Cross to Sunderland service through Arlesey.

Grand Central services are now in the hands of an increased fleet of Class 180 diesel multiple units. On 21 January 2022, 180102, despite the conflicting numbers on its front end, heads towards London as it passes Tempsford.

The same type of units are in use by another competitor operating on the ECML, Hull Trains. As their name implies, they offer an alternative service between Hull and London Kings Cross. On 5 September 2016, 180103 passes Sandy on one of Hull Trains' services.

Passing the same station on 31 October 2017 is sister unit 180113. All LNER, Grand Central and Hull Trains services pass through Bedfordshire without any scheduled station calls.

The majority of LNER services are now in the hands of Azuma units. The Azumas, the name means 'east' in Japanese, were assembled at Hitachi's plant in Newton Aycliffe, close to the ECML at Darlington, following shipment of the bodyshells from Japan. One of their nine-coach sets, 801212, is seen passing Holme Green crossing, south of Biggleswade, in April 2021 on a service from Edinburgh to London.

The fleet also consists of five-car units, often worked in pairs on services between London and Yorkshire. Single units are used on some workings, including a recently introduced service linking Lincoln with London. On 16 July 2020, 800208 passes Tempsford on a service bound for Lincoln.

Further competition for LNER has recently arrived on the ECML in the form of Lumo. Owned by the First Group, Lumo commenced services in September 2021 between Edinburgh and London, with calls at Morpeth, Newcastle and Stevenage. The name Lumo is a combination of the words luminosity (lu) and motion (mo). Their units are similar to that of the Azuma, but without the additional diesel engine. They have a fleet of five units, including 803002 seen here at Tempsford on 21 January 2022 on an Edinburgh to London Kings Cross service.

In addition to these frequent express services passing through the county, the three Bedfordshire stations on the ECML are served by regular stopping services between Peterborough and London. Class 317 electric multiple units were introduced on these services from the early 1980s and were in use for over a quarter of a century. On 5 November 2016, 317337 approaches Sandy on a stopping service to Peterborough.

From 2010, these Class 317 units were joined in service by a fleet of Class 321 units on these ECML services between London and Peterborough. On 3 September 2013, 321410 leaves Biggleswade on a stopping service to Kings Cross.

The use of Class 365 units on Bedfordshire stopping services dates back to the mid-1990s. On 31 October 2017, 365530 and 365532 are paired on a service to London Kings Cross, making their call at Sandy.

On 19 November 2017, 365507 and 365512 are seen stopping at Arlesey heading north on a service to Peterborough.

The electric multiple unit line up was completed by the use of Class 387 Electrostars on local services to Peterborough, although they were mainly used on the route from Kings Cross to Cambridge, Ely and Kings Lynn. On 25 September 2017, 387122 heads south through Tempsford on a Peterborough to Kings Cross service.

The end of 2017 saw a major change in the operation of these stopping services. By this date, these Great Northern services were included in the Govia Thameslink Railway franchise and new eight- and twelve-coach Class 700 units were progressively introduced. On 5 April 2021, 700129 passes Holme Green crossing, south of Biggleswade, on a southbound service.

In 2018, through services commenced using the Canal Tunnels in London, so called because of their proximity to the Regent's Canal. This enabled through running to St Pancras International rather than Kings Cross, and onwards across London to the South Coast. These services now operate half-hourly between Peterborough and Horsham, West Sussex using twelve-coach Class 700 Desiro City units such as 700133, seen here in 2019 heading to Peterborough on a service from the Sussex coast.

The Hornsey-based Class 717 units are a six-car unit similar to their Class 700 counterparts. They make occasional runs on the ECML through the county. On 25 March 2021, for example, 717001 is seen heading south from Peterborough to Hornsey depot on an empty stock movement.

A limited number of freight services pass through Bedfordshire on the ECML. This regular DB Cargo working from Dollands Moor to Scunthorpe is passing Arlesey on 9 October 2020 with 66221, heading north.

On 5 April 2021, it's the turn of 66192 to be in charge of the same working. It approaches Holme Green Crossing with the empty wagons returning to Scunthorpe. This DB Cargo working, which originated at Ebange in eastern France, is one of the few workings regularly using the Channel Tunnel.

Another longstanding freight working within the county is operated by DB Cargo on behalf of Plasmor Brick Company. Regular services operate between Yorkshire, Biggleswade and Bow, East London. On 8 September 2020, 66002 is seen leaving the company's Biggleswade sidings and passing through the station on the return working to Heck, near Selby, in North Yorkshire.

A less frequent DB Cargo working sees a rake of spoil wagons moved from Doncaster to Wembley. Their Class 66 locomotive, 66030, heads south past Tempsford on this southbound service on 2 January 2020.

Most Freightliner services at the southern end of the ECML join and leave at Peterborough and travel across East Anglia to Felixstowe. One exception that operates through the county is the service linking Stourton Terminal, Leeds, with the deep-sea container port at London Gateway. On 8 September 2020, 66534 heads the northbound service to Leeds past Holme Green Crossing.

In common with all main lines in the UK, there's always the chance of a more unusual working passing through the county. On 9 October 2010, for example, two GBRf Class 66 locomotives pass Arlesey with 66710 being dragged to the company's Peterborough depot by sister loco, 66702. The pair were on the move from Ferme Park in North London.

On 18 June 2021, DB Cargo's move from Dollands Moor to Scunthorpe did not involve returning wagons from France. Instead their loco, 66090, was used to move three sister locos to North Lincolnshire for onward movement to the company's main depot at Toton, on the Derbyshire and Nottinghamshire border. The three, 66028, 66190 and 66010, were being repatriated after many years of service in France.

The clock was turned back on 17 June 2017, when A4 Pacific 60009 *Union of South Africa* passed through the county, evoking childhood memories of regularly sighting her working ECML expresses in the early 1960s. The steam engine is accompanied by DB Cargo's 66047 on a move from National Railway Museum in York to Stewarts Lane in South London.

An even longer distance loco movement passed through Bedfordshire on 12 June 2020. A pair of veteran Class 37s, 37116 and 37025, headed north on a light engine move covering almost the entire length of the ECML, from Tonbridge Yard to Oxwellmains, near Dunbar, in Scotland.

Another example of this popular diesel class appeared on 3 March 2022 when 37800 was called on to move two redundant Class 321 electric multiple units from their Clacton depot to Worksop for further storage.

The units involved were 321430 and 321427, nearest the camera. The convoy was seen passing Tempsford crossing.

Heading in the opposite direction on 13 July 2020 are sister units 322484 and 321903. They are in the process of transferring from use by Northern to Greater Anglia (GA). The pair are bound for GA's Clacton depot on a move from Doncaster.

The Network Rail HST also makes regular appearances on the ECML. On 13 July 2020, power cars 43013 and 43062 head south through Tempsford, on the Heaton to Cambridge leg of the diagram.

On 3 January 2022, the pairing of power cars 43251 and 43272, with Cola Rail branding, pass on a Darlington to London Kings Cross working. This New Measurement Train enables Network Rail's engineers to assess the track conditions and identify any places where attention is required.

A variety of other On Track Plant (OTP) regularly pass through the area. On 4 March 2022, Volker Rail's tamper DR75504 heads south on a move from Peterborough to Hitchin.

On 19 January 2020, a Sunday, the worksite was at Tempsford, closing the crossing to road vehicles. Network Rail's Ballast Regulator, DR77909, and Tamper, DR73120, were both in attendance.

Railways in the Bedford Area

Approximately 30 miles of Midland Main Line runs through Bedfordshire, with the town of Bedford itself at the northern end of this stretch. It is also the junction for the surviving branch line to Bletchley, known as the Marston Vale line. In the late 1970s the former Bedford Midland Road station was moved approximately 100 metres to the north. This is the view of the station entrance in March 2022, now accessed from Ashburnham Road.

In the 1980s, trackwork in the Bedford area was realigned to enable Marston Vale services to terminate at Bedford's main station. On 8 November 2016, 150109 is waiting to leave the dedicated bay platform (number 1a) on a service to Bletchley, viewed from the station footbridge.

In addition to the bay platform, there are five through lines and four main platforms in the main station. This rare 'full house' view on 31 October 2016, shows all five lines occupied. From left to right, three Class 700 units, 700107, 700111 and 700015, occupy platforms 1, 2 and 3. HST power car 43081 is passing non-stop using the southbound fast line, while Meridian, 222017, is calling at platform 4 on a northbound service.

Bedford is currently the northern terminus of Govia Thameslink services from Brighton. As a result, the area around the station is a major stabling and servicing point for the company's fleet of electric multiple units. The local sidings were home to four of the fleet of twelve-car Class 700 units on Boxing Day 2016, namely, from left to right, 700106, 700113, 700111 and 700115. In the days of First Capital Connect operation, the sidings were commissioned and named Jowett's Sidings in memory of a local train crew leader, Rodney.

Additional siding capacity is located alongside the Midland Main Line itself. In March 2022, these sidings are home to six of Govia Thameslink's sub-class of eight-car Class 700 units. The sidings are viewed from an arriving Marston Vale service.

Turning the clock back around thirty years, Network SouthEast (NSE) livery was the order of the day in the run up to rail privatisation. In April 1991, these sidings are home to various NSE units, including 319179, 319184 and 319008.

The regular stabling of locomotives at Bedford ceased many years ago. That day in April 1991, 31112 is stabled alongside an unidentified Class 56.

Also present that day was a pair of Class 20s, including 20902. They were stabled between duties on the Hunslet Barclay weedkiller train in use at that time.

An additional siding is located to the north of Bedford station's platform 1. It is able to hold formations of up to eight coaches. On 10 July 2015, a pair of Class 319 units is stabled between duties, with 319216 nearer the buffers.

The two stations in Bedford, Midland (as the main station is often referred) and St Johns, are around a quarter of a mile apart, separated by the River Great Ouse. On 5 September 2020, GBRf's 66770 waits on the river bridge on a Bletchley to Peak Forest working.

Heading in the opposite direction on 28 December 2021 is DB Cargo's 66090. It is waiting to proceed towards St Johns station on a route learner. The station at Bedford St Johns and the line westward is featured in the Marston Vale chapter later in this publication.

As already mentioned, those Marston Vale services to and from Bletchley have used Bedford's main station since the mid-1980s. Diesel multiple units from classes 150 and 153 were the mainstay on these services for many years. On 23 March 2017, single-coach 153366 waits to form a service to Bletchley.

Back in the late 1990s, the line's operator, Silverlink, experienced reliability issues with their first generation diesel units. External help arrived in the shape of a pair of Class 31s hired in from Fragonset Railways to operate two-coach trains, with one loco at each end (top 'n' tailed) to avoid the need for a run round at Bletchley and Bedford. On 28 July 1999, 31452 and 31468 are seen waiting for any customers bound for Bletchley.

In 2019, Marston Vale service operators, London Northwestern Railway, introduced Class 230 diesel units on these workings. On 17 June that year, 230003 waits in Bedford's bay platform forming the 09:29 service to Bletchley.

Three of these two-coach units are in use on these services, each converted by Viva Rail from former London Underground 'D' stock. The seating mix partly reflects their past use and is complemented by a number of local features including background on local stations and history. This is the interior view of sister unit 230004.

Passenger services south on the Midland Main Line across London and to the Sussex Coast have seen a variety of electric unit classes used in recent years. The Class 319 units were the mainstay of these services for almost thirty years. They were built from 1987 onwards and finally withdrawn from Thameslink services in summer 2017. On 13 December 2016, 319009 has just terminated from Brighton.

The Class 319 units were supplemented by use of Class 377 Electrostar units. On 7 September 2016, 377207 waits to leave platform 2 on a southbound service.

The Electrostar Class 387 units entered service with Thameslink from 2015 onwards but have since been completely displaced by Class 700 units and transferred to Great Northern services. On 8 September 2015, 387106 is one of a pair of units on a service from Bedford to Brighton.

A slippage in delivery schedule for Class 700 units resulted in Class 387/2 units, intended for Gatwick Express services, seeing use on Thameslink services as a stopgap. On 19 April 2016, 387203 awaits departure from platform 1.

Longer-distance Midland Main Line services from London St Pancras International to Nottingham and Sheffield pass through the county. These services were operated by Stagecoach from 2007 to 2019, under the East Midlands Trains branding. On 10 December 2017, following a light snowfall, HST power car 43044 is on the rear of a service as it heads north from Bedford, bound for Nottingham.

These HSTs were to notch up almost forty years' service on the Midland Main Line, from 1982 to 2021. For the last three years, they were operated by East Midlands Railway (EMR), owned by Abellio. Latterly, the company used refurbished HSTs transferred from LNER operations on the East Coast Main Line. On the last evening in service, 15 May 2021, InterCity-liveried power car 43102 passes Oakley, a couple of miles north of Bedford.

On 21 June 2020, a few miles to the north, 43048 and 43049 are seen passing through the Bedfordshire countryside near Souldrop, close to the county boundary with Northamptonshire.

A couple of months earlier, in March 2021, EMR-liveried power cars 43310 and 43274 are seen passing Oakley on an out and back empty coaching stock working from St Pancras.

Since 2004, the veteran HSTs have been joined by a fleet of twenty-seven Class 222 diesel units, known as Meridians. On 3 July 2018, seven-car Meridian 222001 heads north through Oakley on a Sheffield service. There were two village stations to the north of Bedford. Oakley's village station was closed in 1958 and Sharnbrook, a little further north, closed two years later.

Sister seven-car unit 222003 passes another Meridian, four-car 222103, just north of Bedford station, with 60021 in the background waiting a path through the station's platforms. This was the view from Bromham Road bridge, taken on 26 September 2017 before electrification progressed north from Bedford.

Until recently, the five-car variants were the mainstay of Meridian stopping services through the county. On 2 February 2017, 222020 calls at Bedford on a service to London St Pancras International.

A small fleet of four-car Meridians were transferred from Hull Trains in 2009. On 16 November 2017, 222102 overhauls Colas Rail's 70811. The Meridian is heading for London, while the Class 70 has had a much longer journey. The working from Oxwellmains, near Dunbar in Scotland, to West Thurrock in Essex is one of the longest, if not the longest, freight working in the UK.

Following withdrawal of EMR's fleet of HSTs, four former Hull Trains Class 180 units were part of the new order on passenger services from 2021. Just prior to their introduction to service, 180109 passes Oakley on a driver training run on 5 May that year.

The electrification was extended northwards from Bedford as far as Kettering on the Midland Main Line and then along the branch line to Corby. EMR Connect branding was applied to the stopping services between London and Corby. Another driver training run on 1 April 2021 passes Bedford with 360105 and 360101. They were working between Kettering and Kentish Town.

A regular half-hourly service is now operated between London and Corby using the fleet of twenty-one Class 360 electric multiple units that had themselves been displaced on Greater Anglia services. On 7 February 2022, 360109 calls at Bedford on a Corby to London service. The unit had recently been outshopped in EMR Connect's purple livery.

Bedfordshire sees a regular flow of charter trains on the Midland Main Line. They include charters between London Victoria and Chesterfield for nearby Chatsworth House. On 22 June 2016, 67015 is leading, with 67018 on the rear, leaving Bedford on the northbound run.

No locomotive can be responsible for drawing bigger crowds than the iconic 60103 *Flying Scotsman*. On 25 June 2016, it steams away from her Bedford call on a London Victoria to York charter, towards a bridge full of enthusiasts and cameras.

Veteran Brush Type 4 Class 47 diesel locomotive, 47580, brings up the rear of the charter as the train heads north towards Bedford North Junction.

Six months later and it's the turn of LMS Coronation Class 46233 *Duchess of Sutherland* to head north from Bedford. In December 2016, its destination is also York, the charter having commenced its journey from Ealing Broadway.

Another Brush Type 4 diesel locomotive is bringing up the rear. West Coast Railway Company's 47854 is partnering the *Duchess* as the train heads north.

The Bedfordshire section of the Midland Main Line sees regular freight traffic with much of it passing throughout the night. Daytime freight traffic is less predictable with aggregate workings dominating. The majority of these are empty wagons returning to quarries in the Midlands and North West of England. On 11 February 2017, DB Cargo's 66119 heads for the Leicestershire quarry of Mountsorrel on a working from Radlett, Hertfordshire.

Tarmac's concrete plant at Elstow, on the southern outskirts of Bedford, is also served by rail via a spur from the Midland Main Line. On the morning of 3 March 2017, 66086 has just commenced its return journey to Mountsorrel.

For many years, DB Cargo also handled the aggregate traffic between Bletchley and the Derbyshire quarry at Dove Holes, Peak Forest. On 5 September 2014, their Class 60 loco, 60001, heads north on the returning empty wagons for Peak Forest.

The substantial Derbyshire quarry at Tunstead is located close to Peak Forest, with the majority of its rail workings in the hands of Freightliner. On 11 July 2016, a loaded train heads south towards Bedford station hauled by 66621. The delivery is destined for West Thurrock in Essex.

Freightliner also handle traffic to and from Earles Sidings, in Derbyshire's Hope Valley. The sidings are close to the adjacent cement works at Hope. On 15 May 2017, 66623 pulls away from a crew change in Bedford station. The loco is returning to Earles Sidings following unloading at Theale, in Berkshire.

Most of the major freight operators can be seen regularly on the Bedfordshire stretch of the Midland Main Line. By far the rarest is Direct Rail Services with no regular booked workings. On 19 February 2018, however, their Class 66 loco, 66422, made a rare appearance on a weekend engineering train following a possession at Kettering North Junction. The loco is passing Oakley in order to run round at Bedford St Johns and then head northwards back to Whitemoor Yard in Cambridgeshire.

Automotive traffic has made a welcome return to the Midland Main Line in 2022. DB Cargo has constructed a new loading and unloading plant within its extensive site at Toton, on the Derbyshire and Nottinghamshire border for import and export of Toyota cars. On 9 March 2022, 66012 passes Oakley on a working to Dollands Moor, loaded with over 200 of their Corolla models for France and the Czech Republic. Their Aygo and Yaris models are carried in the opposite direction.

Network Rail related movements are commonplace on this section of the MML. On 16 December 2020, Colas Rail's 37219 is seen returning to Derby on a light engine move from Hoo Junction Yard in Kent.

Another popular working involves the use of Network Rail's Inspection Saloon, *Caroline*. On 4 September 2014, it heads through Bedford with Direct Rail Services' 37402 providing the power for the Saloon's duties in the London area.

Light engine positioning moves are inevitable for all rail operators. On 18 September 2015, it's the turn of Freightliner's veteran Class 47 machine, 47830, on one such move from their depot at Leeds to Eastleigh.

Another veteran, albeit with a new identity, appeared on 25 January 2022. The former Class 56 loco, 56069, was originally built in 1979. It has since been rebuilt as a GBRf-owned Class 69 loco, numbered 69004, and was heading from Wellingborough to Tonbridge en route to Eastleigh for a repaint.

Another GBRf favourite was involved in an electric multiple unit move on 18 December 2020. 50049 approaches Bedford on a working to Bletchley. This diesel originally entered service in 1968.

The depot at Bletchley was also the destination of this Freightliner working in July 2016. Their Class 66, 66555, is seen heading south on the MML dragging 387133 from Derby to Bletchley via the Marston Vale line.

Midland Main Line Southwards from Bedford to Luton

To the south of Bedford, the MML runs past the sites of Govia Thameslink's depot at Cauldwell, Tarmac's complex at Elstow and the proposed new station at Wixams – the latter being approximately 3 miles from Bedford. A few miles further south, the four-track railway enters Ampthill Tunnels. On 10 June 2021, East Midlands Railway's Meridian 222020 approaches the tunnel's northern bore on a service to St Pancras.

On the same day, Thameslink eight-car unit 700057 also approaches the tunnel entrance with an empty stock working from Bedford's Cauldwell depot. The twelve-car sub-class form most of the scheduled passenger services to the north of Luton.

On 3 August 2021, GB Railfreight (GBRf)'s 66720 is seen leaving the tunnel on one of the few freight workings that operates through to Central London on the MML. It has delivered its load from Ketton Cement Works, in Lincolnshire, to the terminal at Churchyard Sidings at St Pancras. The returning empty wagons have just exited the tunnels beyond.

In June the same year, GBRf sister loco 66748 is seen heading north with a pair of Southeastern units, 466028 and 466029, in tow. The working from Southeastern's depot at Slade Green, Dartford, to Doncaster Wabtec Works had been diverted via the MML because of engineering work closing its usual route from Kings Cross.

Another diversion during the same engineering work involved Hull Trains services from the Yorkshire city being routed to St Pancras rather than Kings Cross. Their Paragon unit, 802303, approaches the tunnels heading to London.

On 10 June 2021, DB Cargo's 66078 has just commenced its northbound return journey following an earlier aggregates delivery to Luton's Limbury Road terminal. The rake of empty wagons is now being returned to Peak Forest in Derbyshire.

GBRf's small fleet of Class 73 electro-diesels are also frequent visitors to the MML through Bedfordshire. On 13 August 20121, 73964 is seen heading south on a light engine move from Brush Traction's workshops at Loughborough to the company's base at Tonbridge, in Kent.

The station at Ampthill, once situated half a mile to the south of the tunnels, was closed as long ago as 1959. The town's residents nearest alternative MML station is at Flitwick, 2 miles away. It is the first station south of Bedford and 10 miles from the county town. This view shows Flitwick station building and entrance today.

The station can accommodate Thameslink twelve-car electric multiple units with Bedford to Gatwick Airport or Brighton services calling every fifteen minutes. This is the view of the four-platform station with most of these services using the two far, slow line platforms.

The village of Westoning is located a mile or two south of Flitwick offering a rural view of the railway across open fields. In June 2021, Thameslink twelve-car unit 700137 heads for London and the South Coast through the pleasing Bedfordshire countryside.

During the pandemic, East Midlands Railway's Class 360 units were becoming a regular sight as driver training was carried out ahead of their full introduction on the Corby to London services. Their unit, 360110, passes Westoning on one such training run. At the time, the unit retained its original Greater Anglia colour with EMR Connect vinyls applied.

The station at Harlington is 3 miles south of Flitwick, on the outskirts of the village of the same name. As can be seen in this June 2021 view, the station's platform layout is similar to that of Flitwick.

Thameslink services also call at Harlington four times an hour in both directions, while East Midlands Railway services do not. On 17 August 2019, their Meridian, 222007, passes Harlington platform at speed on a Nottingham to London St Pancras service.

4½ miles from Harlington, the MML reaches Leagrave. Originally serving Leagrave village, the station now finds itself in a northern suburb of Luton, offering a choice of stations for travellers from the town. The original Midland station buildings, seen here in 2022, were restored in the 1980s and remain virtually unchanged.

Thameslink's calling frequency at Leagrave is also four times an hour in each direction. On 15 March 2022, their twelve-car unit, 700138, makes a call on a Brighton service.

The main town station at Luton is a couple of a miles south of Leagrave. It is just under 20 miles from Bedford, and 30 miles from Central London. Despite a population of over 200,000 people, the town no longer benefits from longer-distance express services calling here. On 11 November 2021, EMR Meridian 222004 passes through on a high-speed service to London. The town's bus interchange is located adjacent to the rail station, to the right of this photo.

The town's station is regularly served by the four Thameslink trains between Bedford and Brighton each hour, as well as the two EMR Connect services between Corby and London St Pancras. Additionally, a further Thameslink route operates south from here with a half-hourly service to Sutton in Surrey. On 19 April 2016, 319214 is seen leaving on one of these services.

During the autumn leaf fall season the MML, in common with most of the UK rail network, sees regular operation of Rail Head Treatment Trains aimed at improving adhesion on the tracks. On 11 November 2021, DB Cargo Class 66 locomotives 66111 and 66121 are paired on one of these workings. They operate in a top 'n' tail formation, covering all MML lines through Bedfordshire. Operating from the company's Toton depot, the pair are about to layover at Luton on a northbound working.

A stone unloading terminal is located just to the south of Luton station, at Crescent Road. On 2 October 2015, Freightliner's 66601 had earlier brought a loaded train from Mountsorrel Quarry in Leicestershire. Following unloading, the loco is now shunting the wagons in preparation for the return journey.

In 1999, a new station was opened at Luton Airport Parkway, a mile to the south of the main Luton station, serving London Luton Airport. A Direct Air–Rail Transit (DART) is promised between the rail station and the airport terminal building. In the interim, shuttle bus remains in operation. There always seems to be some construction work going on at the station, as this 2019 view shows. To the south of here, the MML crosses the county boundary into Hertfordshire before the next station, Harpenden.

Bedford to Bletchley – Marston Vale Branch

This branch line, lying predominantly within the county of Bedfordshire, is the surviving section of the original Varsity line linking the university cities of Oxford and Cambridge. In this chapter, our journey along the branch will trace the route, broadly south-westward from Bedford. The first station is at Bedford St Johns. Its spartan, single platform station is seen here in October 2016.

As I write these notes, the finer details of the proposed East West Rail project are not clear, so I have restricted commentary to the present 16-mile-long branch, its stations and services in Bedfordshire. Following privatisation, a decade of Silverlink operation ended in 2007 with London Midland taking over services. Just prior to the end of their tenure, two-car Class 150 diesel unit 150107 approaches St Johns on the single-track half-mile-long spur linking Bedford's two stations.

This single-track section was home to DB Cargo's 66054 on 18 November 2018. The loco was involved in a weekend track possession between Bedford's two stations.

One of the Marston Vale's few regular freight diagrams involves the return of the empty hoppers from the earlier Peak Forest to Bletchley stone working. These wagons are returned to Peak Forest or, as in the case here, at weekends they often layover in Wellingborough Yard. On 15 May 2021, 66713 passes through St Johns station heading for Wellingborough.

West of Bedford St Johns station, the branch becomes a double-track railway. The next station is Kempston Hardwick, 3 miles from St Johns. It is the least used station on the line, escaping closure on several occasions last century. This is the view looking towards Bedford on 25 August 2020.

By August 2020, services were being operated by London Northwestern Railways using a pool of three Class 230 units. These units were developed by Viva Rail, using aluminium bodyshells of former London Underground 'D' stock. Originally built by Metro Cammell, they date back to 1980. Unit number 230003 calls on 1608 departure to Bletchley.

On 7 April 2021, GB Railfreight's 66708 is in charge of the empty hoppers returning from Bletchley. On this occasion, the loco worked the rake directly back to the Derbyshire quarry.

The Marston Vale offers a convenient link between the Midland Main Line and West Coast Main Line when moving empty coaching stock or units. On 10 January 2021, 47727 hauls new Greater Anglia unit 720549 from Wolverton back to the Rail Innovation & Test Centre, near Melton Mowbray.

The next station, Stewartby, is just a mile and a half further west. The village was originally established to house the workers at the London Brick Company. At its peak around fifty years ago, the brickworks produced in excess of 700 million bricks per year. Sadly, the brick works here closed in 2008. On 8 June 2020, 230004 approaches the station on a Bletchley-bound service.

As already mentioned, the Class 230 units displaced the Class 150 and Class 153 combinations on the branch. On 12 November 2016, single car 153356 calls on a service to Bedford.

Back in 2016, the Peak Forest to Bletchley and return workings were in the hands of DB Cargo. On 12 November that year, 66182 passes Stewartby with the returning empties from Bletchley. On this occasion, a Saturday, the train was destined for Doncaster Belmont Yard for weekend stabling.

On 26 July 2019, a one-off Freightliner wagon positioning move made use of the branch. Their loco, 66606, is seen heading towards Bletchley and the WCML on a working from Woodhouse Junction, near Sheffield, to Brentford, Middlesex.

On 9 April 2021, a pair of DC Rail Class 60 locos were called upon to return new unit, 730101, from Wembley Yard to Derby. Loco 60028 is seen leading the train.

Bringing up the rear is sister loco, 60046. The new five-car Class 730 electric multiple unit is for future use with London Northwestern Railway.

Another variation of loco classes was used on 8 June 2020, when 57310 was paired with 37608 on this new unit move. The ensemble were working from the Melton Test Centre to Willesden. They were delivering unit 710130 to London Overground.

The same Class 37 loco was in use a few days earlier, on 2 June, when 37608 was used to drag new Crossrail unit number 345026. The unit had been in storage at Worksop and was being delivered to Crossrail's depot at Old Oak in West London.

The station at Millbrook lies just under a mile and a half from Stewartby, but is around 2 miles from the small village of the same name. This is the 2017 view of the Bletchley-bound platform at the station.

The station is also a couple of miles from the much larger community of Marston Moretaine. On the opposite platform, in 2021, a bench was unveiled in memory of Captain Sir Tom Moore, one of Marston Moretaine's notable residents and a hero during the Covid pandemic.

The station at Lidlington lies a further mile and a quarter from Millbrook. On 25 August 2020, 230003 approaches the station.

The same unit achieved more success in terms of custom on 13 August 2021. It is making a call on an early afternoon service to Bedford.

Also on 13 August 2020, another new unit was heading in the opposite direction, with 56081 leading Greater Anglia unit 720571.

This time it's the turn of GB Railfreight's Class 66 locomotive 66767 to be found on the rear. The unit was being moved from Derby to Wembley.

Ridgmont station is the next call on the line, 2 miles west of Lidlington. The nearby former brickworks site is now a large Amazon warehouse. This 2016 view of Ridgmont station was taken through the front window of a Class 150 unit heading towards Bedford. The old station building here is now a working museum, education centre and coffee shop.

When a full rail service is in operation, services often pass each other around the station area here. This was the case on 15 March 2019, when 153356 and 150109 were the two units operating branch services.

The Marston Vale Community Rail Partnership and the Bedford–Bletchley Rail Users' Association have both put considerable effort in promoting increased patronage on the line. A 2022 initiative saw two of the Class 230 units having a 'Greensand Country' makeover, as seen in this bodyside promotion on 230003. The name is taken from the Greensand Ridge, which runs across this part of Bedfordshire.

Unfortunately, this view of 150105 highlights the fragility of Marston Vale line performance. The unit was unexpectedly terminated at Ridgmont on this evening peak service from Bletchley. Worse, customers were then left to make their own ongoing travel arrangements, while the unit returned empty coaching stock to Bletchley.

On 12 March 2016, DB Cargo's 66200 takes the curve through Ridgmont station with the returning empties from Bletchley to Peak Forest.

Occasional infrastructure workings traverse the line. On 8 January 2017, DB Cargo's 66068 heads through Ridgmont on a return working from Willesden to Bescot. The reason for its routing via the Marston Vale line is unknown.

On 14 April 2018, Freightliner's 66614 made an appearance along the branch. It is seen passing through Ridgmont with a rake of empty hoppers from Bletchley to Barrow Hill, near Chesterfield.

Another empty stock move on 18 December 2016 saw a Southeastern Class 375 electric multiple unit, 375907 hauled by 37800. The unit had left their Ramsgate depot and was being dragged to Derby.

A further one and a half miles west lies the station of Aspley Guise. This is a 2019 view of the station's staggered platforms looking towards Bletchley.

Aspley Guise is another of the least used stations within Bedfordshire. On 26 August 2019, 230003 calls on an early afternoon service to Bedford. Regrettably, no customers boarded or alighted.

The final Bedfordshire station on the Marston Vale line is Woburn Sands. It is 12 miles from Bedford, and just 4 miles from the line's terminus at Bletchley. This is the view looking towards Bletchley on 12 July 2018. The gentleman watering the plants is another example of the care shown by the local communities along the line.

The local community involvement is also shown here by the 'Welcome to Woburn Sands' display. This has been created by the pupils of years 7 and 8 at Fulbrook Middle School. Beyond Woburn Sands, the line crosses the county boundary with stations at Bow Brickhill and Fenny Stratford before terminating at Bletchley.

Leighton Buzzard on the West Coast Main Line (WCML)

A short stretch of the WCML runs through Bedfordshire in the area around Leighton Buzzard and Linslade, approximately 40 miles to the north-west of London Euston. This is the 2022 view of Leighton Buzzard station building and entrance.

The station today consists of four platforms, with most stopping services calling at platforms 3 and 4. It was once a junction station, with a branch to Dunstable and onwards to Luton. These trains used a bay platform to the right of this view looking north. Closure to passengers came with the Beeching Axe in the mid-1960s, with freight at the Luton end lingering on for another two decades.

Since rail privatisation, longer-distance services have been in the hands of Virgin Trains and, more recently, Avanti. A constant procession of these services pass through the Leighton Buzzard and Linslade area every few minutes. In October 2020, Avanti-liveried Pendolino 390152 has just emerged from Linslade Tunnel on a northbound service.

Heading in the opposite direction on the same day is sister Pendolino 390119. The distinctive 'Pride' livery reflects Avanti West Coast's commitment to the LGBTQ+ community across its network. Their services connect London with the West Midlands, North West England, North Wales and Scotland.

A commemoration of a very different kind is reflected in this view of Avanti Pendolino, 390042. Its face mask front end is a visual reminder of the times rail services lived through during the Covid pandemic.

Avanti's fleet of Pendolinos operate the majority of their services, complimented by a smaller fleet of diesel-powered Voyagers. On 13 October 2020, 221106 and 221111 are paired to make a ten-coach train on a service from London to the West Midlands.

Leighton Buzzard is served by stopping trains operated by London Northwestern Railway. Their Class 350 electric multiple units operate between London, Milton Keynes, Northampton and Birmingham. On 27 January 2022, 350107 and 350374 meet in the station.

These four-car units usually operate in eight-car formations. On 20 May 2021, 350122 leads an eight-car service passing Old Linslade on a Northampton to London Euston service.

Sister unit 350376 is leading on a service heading north to Milton Keynes Central. It has just emerged from the 300-yard-long Linslade Tunnel, about half a mile north of Leighton Buzzard station. Linslade Woods occupy the area above.

Leighton Buzzard is also served by Southern services between Milton Keynes Central, Clapham Junction and East Croydon, usually formed of a pair of Class 377 electric multiple units. In May 2020, 377209 leads on a southbound service.

The WCML around Leighton Buzzard sees a number of On Track Plant movements through the area. One such example was the appearance of Network Rail's newly delivered Milling Machine. Numbered DR79105 and DR79104, it is seen heading south through the station heading for Plasser's works at West Ealing.

The WCML also sees regular movements of the Royal Mail's Class 325 postal units. On 20 May 2021, 325004 passes Old Linslade on a move from Crewe to Willesden.

Despite the frequency of both express and stopping passenger services, this southern end of the WCML sees regular freight workings operated by all of the major railfreight operators. The WCML sees container trains to and from the UK's three largest ports handling such traffic, namely Felixstowe, London Gateway and Southampton. In January 2022, Freightliner's 66539 rounds the curve to the south of Leighton Buzzard on a Felixstowe to Lawley Street, Birmingham service.

These Class 66 stalwarts have now been working these container trains for over twenty years. Freightliner's 66517 passes Old Linslade on a southbound container service. This particular loco was built in the year 2000.

Rail accounts for 30 per cent of all container throughput at the port of Felixstowe, with that figure rising to around 50 per cent of all traffic to the North and West Midlands. Despite the option of routing via Peterborough and across East Anglia, most traffic between Lawley Street, Birmingham and Felixstowe passes through Leighton Buzzard. Freightliner's 66532 is seen here heading from Birmingham to Felixstowe.

Some Freightliner aggregates traffic uses the Bedfordshire WCML. Here, 66602 emerges from Linslade Tunnel on a return working of empty box wagons from Willesden to Tunstead Quarry.

One of the regular traffic flows through the Channel Tunnel consists of a rake of cargowagons from France to Daventry International Rail Freight Terminal (DIRFT) in Northamptonshire, usually via a layover in Wembley Yard. On 20 May 2021, 66013 is passing Old Linslade on its way to Daventry.

These DB Cargo workings handle bottled water imported from France and delivered to DIRFT for onward distribution. On 27 January 2022, it's the turn of 66185 to haul the northbound service through Leighton Buzzard.

GB Railfreight also use the WCML for some of their container services from Felixstowe. Their Class 66 loco, 66772, is seen passing Old Linslade on a service to Associated British Ports' container terminal at Hams Hall near Birmingham.

Direct Rail Services also operate container traffic through Bedfordshire, on services to and from DIRFT on behalf of Tesco. 66302 is seen through Old Linslade on a southbound working from Daventry to Tilbury.

Freightliner continues to make use of electric traction on some of its services. It operates a pool of Class 90 locomotives, which commonly operate in pairs to and from Ipswich. The branch beyond Ipswich towards Felixstowe remains non-electrified, requiring a change of traction at Ipswich. This service from Trafford Park, Manchester, to Felixstowe is powered by 90041 and 90011 between Crewe and Ipswich.

Light engine moves through Leighton Buzzard are frequent occurrences. On 27 January 2022, it's the turn of Freightliner's 90015 to run southbound from Crewe to Wembley.

As well as their container traffic, Direct Rail Services (DRS) also operate automotive traffic between Dagenham and Garston, Merseyside. The traffic, a joint operation with STVA UK, is for their customer, Ford. On this occasion, the power is provided by 66425.

Much to the delight of rail enthusiasts, this working occasionally sees alternative power in the form of one of DRS's pool of ten Class 88 bi-mode locomotives. On 20 May 2021, 88009 is seen exiting Linslade Tunnel and heading northwards for Merseyside.